The Quigmans

Tunnel of Just Friends

By Buddy Hickerson

Four Walls Eight Windows
New York/London

FIRST EDITION AUGUST 1996

PUBLISHED in the United States by
FOUR WALLS EIGHT WINDOWS
39 West 14th Street, Suite 503
New York, NY 10011

U.K. offices:
FOUR WALLS EIGHT WINDOWS/TURNAROUND
27 HORSELL ROAD LONDON, N5 1XL, ENGLAND

LIBRARY of CONGRESS CATALOGING-IN-PUBLICATION Data:

Hickerson, Buddy. The Quigmans: tunnel of just friends:
cartoons / by Buddy Hickerson -- 1st ed. p. cm.
ISBN 1-56858-100-9 (paper)
1. American wit and humor, Pictorial. I. Title
NC 1429. H48A4 1996
741. 5'973--dc20   96-23881
                     CIP

My WEB Site:

http://quigmans.com

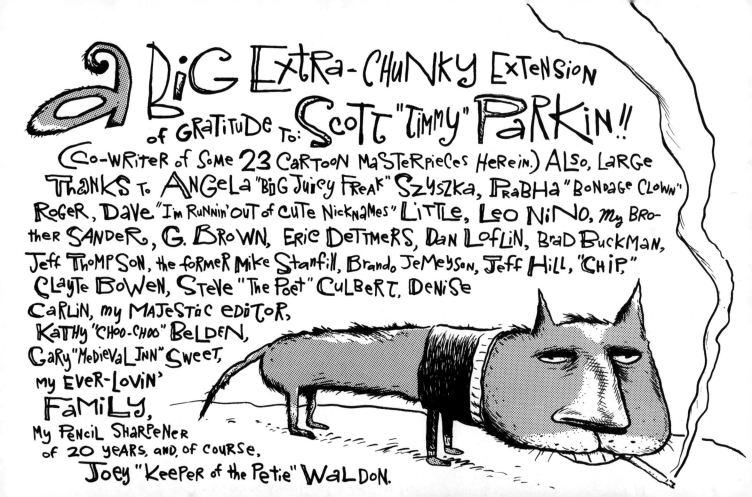

A BIG EXTRA-CHUNKY EXTENSION of GRATITUDE TO: SCOTT "TIMMY" PARKIN!! (CO-WRITER of SOME 23 CARTOON MASTERPIECES HEREIN.) ALSO, LARGE THANKS TO ANGELA "BIG JUICY FREAK" SZYSZKA, PRABHA "BONDAGE CLOWN" ROGER, DAVE "I'M RUNNIN' OUT OF CUTE NICKNAMES" LITTLE, LEO NINO, MY BROTHER SANDER, G. BROWN, ERIC DETTMERS, DAN LOFLIN, BRAD BUCKMAN, JEFF THOMPSON, the FORMER MIKE STANFILL, BRANDO JEMEYSON, JEFF HILL, "CHIP," CLAYTE BOWEN, STEVE "THE POET" CULBERT, DENISE CARLIN, MY MAJESTIC EDITOR, KATHY "CHOO-CHOO" BELDEN, GARY "MEDIEVAL INN" SWEET, MY EVER-LOVIN' FAMILY, MY PENCIL SHARPENER of 20 YEARS, AND, OF COURSE, JOEY "KEEPER OF THE PETIE" WALDON.

FRANCINE DISCOVERS THE 5 STAGES of DATING BOB: DENIAL, ANGER, CONFUSION, NAUSEA AND FINALLY, ACCEPTANCE of the CHECK.

SORRY

WHAM!

Francine's virtue is saved from a reckless advance with the deployment of her first-date air bag.

"Some hunters like a challenge, Stan, but not me!"

The vibramode on Bob's pager was his only friend.

"This honey is screamin' your name—a 1986 street cleaner! You can only drive it on Tuesdays and Thursdays, but baby . . . it hugs the curb!"

Bob achieves a runner's high.

"I like to think I can judge a man by the car he drives, Bob. Yours, to me, says: 'Fear of commitment.'"

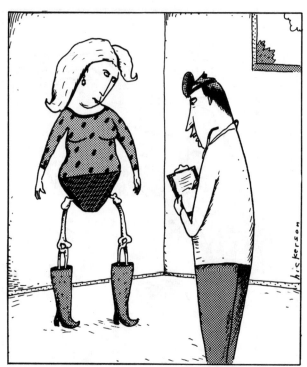

"This time, let's go with a lower concentration of the thigh cream, Ms. Quigman."

"During surgery, you'll be in good hands with Dr. Scruffy. He's our bone specialist."

"Honey . . . I'm mighty proud of you! This cake of yours is really moist!"

"Mom! I found a crippled baby bird in the woods. . . . It makes me laugh."

"For the last time, it's *not* mange!
It's male-pattern baldness!"

"Who ordered the po' boy?"

"All those in disagreement with me signify by saying, 'So long gainful employment.'"

"Mighty proud of that one, Jed. Nailed her in
midcigarette break behind a TV station."

"Try and calm down, ma'am. Now just exactly how was the steak smothered?"

TIMES WERE SO BLEAK THAT THE ONLY WAY BOB COULD EXPERIENCE A WARM FUZZY WAS TO CLEAN OUT HIS LINT TRAP.

"So I, like, gave up seeking Nirvana. . . . I can't even find tickets to their concert! Thank you. Seriously, folks . . . Take my waif, please!"

"Yes! That's him, officer! That's the guy who
stole my spotlight!"

"Your wedding announcement's in the paper, Bob. But the bride's name has been withheld, pending notification of next of kin."

"So if you'd like to go out with your stepmom . . . we'll pay for it!"

"Me and the plate of donuts hit it off real good, Chuck. I just hope they don't run out like my exhusband."

As Bob aged, he minimized the embarrassment
of his ear hair by fashioning it into
swanky sideburns.

"And the winner . . . by a stroke!"

The Drivers License Photo of Dorian Gray.

"... and I just want that punk Barney to know ... he's *next!* Can you say *extinct?* I knew that you could!"

Camping with a hack writer.

The writing of the Declaration of Codependency.

Bob was unclear on the whole disposable
camera idea.

Bob and Francine's "couple baby talk" was cute and endearing, but sooner or later . . . they needed more.

"Oh! So I'm paranoid, eh? Lemme ask you *this*, Mr. Peace-of-Mind: Does the fact that we're called *broilers* mean anything to you?"

Death row beer commercial.

"Okay, Francine . . . We'll start your workout today by stretching out your fingers and releasing that sandwich."

Bad hints from Heloise.

"Hey, Frank! Did anybody turn in this guy's youth?"

Used Car Salesman Marriage Proposal.

"Whadaya expect? He's a muscle-bound mime.
Women love the strong, silent type."

Bob's new-found pride was manifested when he began scraping the "Don't Laugh, It's Paid For" bumper stickers off of everything he owned.

"I know he seems pretty white bread . . . but I hear he has a dark side."

"Nasty razor burn there, Bob. . . ."

When doctors fight.

"No, no. You misunderstand me, my dear. I didn't say I was a philanthropist. I said I was a philanderer . . . with a *lisp.*"

* Based on an actual fact!

After his human mating technique fails, Bob tries the traditional, love-snaring neck bloat of the common toad.

Bob's long-distance relationship.

"We've all been there, Marcie. The first six steps are the hardest."

"I don't get it. We've been hiding the growth hormones in his brussels sprouts for months and he hasn't grown an inch."

"Okay, kids . . . get out there and break some legs!"

"Sorry I'm late. . . . I was up all night cramming."

What really happens in the women's room at a singles bar.

Bob's friends throw him a surprise pity party.

Martha Stewart and Heloise fight to determine
Helpful-Hint Supremacy.

"Yeah . . . Dis is Victoria. No, we ain't got no more
of da Evening in Bermuda size 8. Fergit it.
Oh, yeah? Well, bite me!"

"AAUGH! It'll take me *weeks* to clean this place up! *Dirt everywhere!!* And as for you, my friend, I have two words: public restroom!"

Steve took the "never let em see you sweat" concept a little too seriously.

* Repressive Celibate and the Seven Politically
Correct Height-Challenged.

"I've come a long way since I was a minority whip. Now I have a Clinton whip, a welfare mother whip, and, of course, my Jesse Helmet."

"I propose we tear down huge areas of the city so we can yell our heads off and hear our voices bounce back!"

Bob is staggered by the realization that women are completely naked underneath their clothes.

A high-strung game of emotional poker.

More American Gladiator rejects.

Being self-employed begins to mess
with Bob's head.

Bob discovers the secret of youth.

"I'd like to join you for bowling night, Pete, but the
wife just said 'Stay,' and I'll be danged
if I can't move a muscle!"

"We don't take kindly to poachers round here mister. We like *our* eggs in a nice omelet."

"Finally, I find myself in a committed relationship."

Gil Bounder forges on with his
"Get Rich Slow Scheme."

"I think I'm gonna make a pass at one of these Indians, Bob. It's not that I don't love you . . . I just don't wanna be tied down."

"Arright, move along, buddy. . . . Nothin' to see here."

"Uh . . . Excuse me! I've got a hair net
in my soup!"

"I'm tellin' ya, Herbie . . . Santa Claus is watching me."

"Hey, Mom! Hey, Dad! I got a divorce and lost my job. Could I stay for a while?"

"Wow! Look what the cat's in drag in!"

Early warning sign of involvement in a
love/hate relationship.

The world's record hair ball was released by a Tippy the Cat of Charles City, Iowa, after she finally laid her paws on a good decongestant.

The pressure is insurmountable when your date comes with on-deck options.

Bob the Magician performs his famous
Amazing Vanishing Elephant Trick.

"Honey! I thought we had the place sprayed for lawyers."

"Whoa! Those last 24 drinks went straight to my head!"

Date with a movie critic.

"A coupla guys was gunned down at Flamboni's Restaurant tonight. You tell anybody where you heard about dis: I'll find you, and I'll kill you."

"See, Bob? The modern ranch isn't at all
like you expected!"

"Excuse me! Are those Tuba Boy jeans you're wearing?"

Bob Quigman had that flamboyant,
seat-of-the-pants sales style.

"Prehistoric pine cleaner real pain to use . . . but
leave lingering country-fresh bouquet."

A scene from *Look Who's Talking Us to Death: The Rush Limbaugh Story.*

"And now, for a wider perspective on that last play, let's go to the blimp."

"Here's a fun item: Hundreds of people die every day . . . and it's never me! Woo! Arright! Gimme five, news babe!"

"You're not showing good progress, Mr. Quigman! You need to let go of some of the things you're holding onto! *Gimme!!*"

Francine induces labor in Bob.

"Thank you, members of the academy."

How the aliens will reveal themselves.

"No! No! You're too kind!"

Sally Jesse James Raphael.

A scene from the discovery of the legendary
Quigman lode of 1994.

"Oh! Well, here it is!"

Bob's interest subsided when he discovered no phone numbers were listed.

"Frankly, all that you can be is not nearly enough."

Thag invents the first tie tack.

"Pine box or plastic?"

Mel's no-pest-strip jumpsuit: a big
summertime favorite.

"What's yer poison, boys?"

Bob makes plans for his nursery school reunion.

Bob is expelled from driving school.

Baseball: The Early Days

Unlike the credit card vouchers he presented to his Denny's customers, Bob's bottom portion was already filled out.

"You watch yerself, Ardell. . . . That old, expired milk'll turn on ya."

Pete regretted putting a quarter in the motel's Magic Finger box.

A stickler for consistency, Chief Edwards insisted
on appropriate uniforms for his *drag*net.

"Well, hey! It's a lucky penny!"